# Où est Bouboul?
# Where is Bouboul?

*By* Opal Dunn
*with* Marilyn Malin

*Illustrated by* Annabel Spenceley

CHERRYTREE BOOKS

A Cherrytree Book

Designed and produced by
A S Publishing

First published 1992
by Cherrytree Press Ltd
a subsidiary of
The Chivers Company Ltd
Windsor Bridge Road
Bath, Avon BA2 3AX

Text Copyright © Opal Dunn 1992

Concept development Copyright © Marilyn Malin
1992

Illustrations Copyright © Annabel Spenceley 1992

Language Consultant: Andrew Davis

British Library Cataloguing in Publication Data
Dunn, Opal
    Où est Bouboul?: Where is Bouboul? –
    (Learn-a-Language Storybook Series)
    I. Title  II. Series
    448.3

ISBN 0 7451 5163 9 Hardcover
ISBN 0 7451 5182 5 Softcover
ISBN 0 7451 5184 1 Softcover & Cassette

Printed and bound in Italy by L.E.G.O. s.p.a., Vicenza

# Speaking French

The best way to speak French, with a French
accent, is to listen to the cassette and try to imitate
it exactly. If you haven't got a cassette, ask
someone who knows French to read the French in
the book for you.

French people use their lips, tongue, throat and
nose in special ways to make French sounds. Some
of the sounds may be new to you. So listen to
French spoken first and read it later. Notice how
different some of the sounds are.

| | |
|---|---|
| Alphabet letters | The names are different in French. Listen to 'h', 'y' and 'u', for example. There are more sounds in French than there are letters in the alphabet. |
| Consonant letters – all except a e i o u | These are often silent at the end of words, so you write them but you don't say them. *deux  trois* |
| Letter g | g followed by e or i has a similar sound to the letter j. Otherwise it is hard. *garage  sage  regarde* |
| Letter h | h is usually silent *huit  heure  homme* but is sometimes said from the throat. |
| Letter j | j is generally soft in French. Say 'jug' in English and then '*je*' and '*jolie*' in French. |
| Letter r | r is made in the throat, not near the front teeth. Say 'red' in English and then '*rouge*' and '*Murielle*' in French. |

Letter e  e at the end of words is almost silent, so you hardly notice it *piscine glace* EXCEPT when it has an 'accent aigu' *é fermé* (see below).
*ei er ez* at the end of a French word is often said like letter *é* with an accent aigu.
*est* is also said like *é*.

Letter u  u has a special sound in French. To get used to saying this sound, say the letter e in English. While saying it, change the shape of your lips from a broad smile to a small hole. Now you are making the sound of the letter u in French.
*tu Murielle Mumu*

Letter y  y by itself has the same sound as the letter i in French. It is like the first sound in the word 'evening'.

---

Some letters have additional marks that tell you how to say them.

Letter c  If there is a little hook below the letter ç (called a cedilla) it shows the sound has changed to an s sound.
*ça français*

Accents above vowel letters – a e i o u – show a change in the letter sound.

Accent aigu  ´   *fermé entrée méchant*

Accent circonflexe  ^   *tête plaît côte à côté*

Accent grave  \`   *là voilà père très*

# Contents

Murielle, Marc and Michel, the three M's, were getting ready to go swimming. Murielle checked to see that they had their bags.

'Have you got your bag?' she asked.

'Yes, and my money,' said Marc.

Michel said, 'And I've got my bag and my money.'

The three M's went to the bus stop and waited for the bus to go to the swimming pool. As the bus turned the corner Michel said,

'Mumu. There's the bus!' Murielle looked and said,

'It's the five.'

'That's good,' Marc added. 'The five goes to the swimming pool.'

The children got on.

'The swimming pool, one ticket, please,' said Marc.

'The swimming pool, two tickets, please,' said Murielle.

'There's one ticket . . . two tickets,' said the bus driver.

Little Michel said, 'Thanks,' as he took them.

As the three M's got near the pool, the bus driver called out,
    'Swimming pool.' Marc looked up.
    'That's the swimming pool!' he said, pointing.
    'Yes! It's the pool,' little Michel repeated.
Before they got off the bus, Murielle asked again,
    'Have you got your bag, Michel?'

On the way to the pool, the three M's passed a shop that sold ice-cream.

'Do you want an ice-cream?' asked Murielle.

'Yes, a chocolate one for me,' said Marc.

'And me,' added Michel, 'a mocha one, Mumu.'

Marc led the way into the shop.

'Good morning!' he said. 'Three ice-creams, please. Chocolate for me.'

'Mocha for me,' said Michel.

'And strawberry for me, please,' added Murielle.

The girl filled the ice-cream cones and counted them as she handed them to the children.

'There's one . . two . . . three. Three ice-creams. That will be . . .' and she worked out how much it cost.

The children walked on, licking their ice-creams.

'Mmm. It's good,' Marc said.

'Yes, it's good,' echoed Murielle and little Michel chipped in,

'I like ice-cream!'

When they got to the pool, Murielle went to buy the tickets.

'Good morning,' she said. 'Three, please.'

'There, three tickets,' said the man, as he gave her the tickets. Michel was leaning against the door into the hall. A poodle was watching him. Michel wondered why.

'Push, Michel,' said Marc.

'Look out! A dog,' shouted Michel as the door opened. In a flash a poodle, trailing his lead behind him, dashed through the open door.

The three M's followed the dog into the hall. A few seconds later the door opened again, and there was the dog's owner.

'Bouboul, Bouboul, come here! Here!' she called. Murielle looked round.

'Where is the dog?' she asked.

'There! There!' shouted Michel, while Marc pointed and said,

'Under the chair.'

'Get hold of the lead. Quick! Quick!' shouted Murielle.

'I can't,' Michel said as he dived to get it. The old lady was still looking where Marc had pointed.

'Bouboul! Where is my dog?' she said. But Bouboul wasn't there. He was enjoying the game! It was Marc who spotted him.

'There, on the chair,' he said.

Bouboul thought this was a great game. He ran off again.

'Bouboul! Bouboul! Where is the dog?' shouted Marc.

'In the locker,' Murielle shouted back. Michel made a dive.

'I've got it. I've got it,' he said, grabbing the lead.

'Naughty Bouboul!' said the old lady. 'Now behave!'

14

The old lady was happy now Bouboul was caught.

    'Thank you. Thank you very much.' She turned to Murielle.

    'And you. What's your name?' she asked. Murielle replied,

    'My name's Murielle. Murielle Leroux.'

    'My name is Marc.'

    'And me, my name is Michel Leroux.'

'Wait a minute,' the old lady said, as she searched in her bag, looking for her camera.

'A photo: the three M's and Bouboul!

'Michel, take Bouboul. Bouboul behave! Go in front of Michel. Murielle go behind Michel. And you, Marc, go next to Michel. That's it.

*Les trois M's et Barbou*

'One . . . two . . . three . . . Smile!'

'*Ouistiti!*' shouted the three M's together. And, as an enormous smile spread across each face, the camera went 'click'.

# Games to play

*Où est le cadeau?* **Where's the present?**

*Où?*
Where?

| *le cadeau* | *ici* | *là* |
|---|---|---|
| the present | here | there |

*C'est ici.*
It's here.

*C'est là.*
It's there.

*dans le sac*
in the bag

*sur la chaise*
on the chair

*sous la chaise*
under the chair

## How to play

Everyone shuts their eyes except for one person who hides *le cadeau* and says, '*Où est le cadeau?*'

Whoever finds it is the winner and says, '*C'est là* or *C'est ici.*' The winner hides *le cadeau* next time.

## *Murielle dit*　**Murielle says**

*Va devant Bouboul.*
Go in front of Bouboul.

*Va derrière Bouboul.*
Go behind Bouboul.

*Va à côté de Bouboul.*
Go next to Bouboul.

*Je ne peux pas.*
I can't.

Who won?

**How to play**

Choose one player to be Murielle and one to be Bouboul.

Murielle tells the other players what to do in French, for example:

'*Murielle dit va devant Bouboul,*' or '*Murielle dit va à côté de Bouboul.*'

If they do the wrong thing or if they move without her saying, '*Murielle dit,*' they are out.

The last one wins and is Murielle next time.

# A song to sing

Dites avec nous.
Say with us.

Chantez avec nous.
Sing with us.

1    un
     kilomètre

Un kilomètre à pied,
ça use, ça use.
Un kilomètre à pied,
ça use les souliers.

2    deux
     kilomètres

Deux kilomètres à pied,
ça use, ça use.
Deux kilomètres à pied,
ça use les souliers.

Combien?
How many?
How much?

1 un
2 deux
3 trois
4 quatre
5 cinq
6 six
7 sept
8 huit
9 neuf
10 dix
50 cinquante
100 cent

quatre 4 kilomètres

cinquante 50 kilomètres

trois 3 kilomètres

cent 100 kilomètres

Trois kilomètres à pied,
ça use, ça use.
Trois kilomètres à pied,
ça use les souliers.

Cent kilomètres à pied,
ça use, ça use.
Cent kilomètres à pied,
ça use les souliers.

Cent kilomètres
100 kilometres

à pied
on foot

ça use
it wears out

les souliers.
the shoes.

21

# Talking to each other

22

# Rhymes and sums

*Un, deux, trois,*
*Trois, trois, trois.*
*Un pour moi,*
*Et deux pour toi.*

One, two, three,
Three, three, three.
One for me,
And two for you.

Je m'appelle Murielle. — I am called Murielle.
*Comment t'appelles-tu?* — What is your name?
*A B C D arrête.* — A B C D stop.
*Je m'appelle Danielle.* — I am called Danielle.

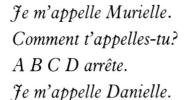

*Mmm. C'est bon.*
*En veux-tu une?*
*Oui ou non?*
*Mmm. C'est bon.*

Mmm. It's good.
Do you want one?
Yes or no?
Mmm. It's good.

*cinq et cinq font dix*          5 + 5 = 10

50 + 50 = 100

cinquante et cinquante font cent

$2 + 2 = 4$

quatre et quatre font huit

$4 + 4 = 8$

# *Talking puppets*

Trace the puppets and colour them in.

Cut out all the pictures and stick them on card.

Ask someone to help you cut two holes in each.

Put your thumb and a finger, or two fingers, through the holes.

Tie a string round Bouboul's neck to make his lead.

Make your puppets talk French, using the words on pages 22/23.

# Saying it right

**Whose bag is it?**   **Whose ice-cream is it?**

In French, words for things and people are either:

     Masculine  *mon sac*    *ton sac*    *un sac*    *le sac*

*or*  Feminine  *ma glace*   *ta glace*   *une glace*  *la glace*

They have got to be one or the other and there are some surprises!

English isn't like that.

# Is it one or is it two?

In French, there are words for one and words for more than one, just as there are in English.

| | | | |
|---|---|---|---|
| *un billet* | *le billet* | *une glace* | *la glace* |
| *deux billets* | *les billets* | *deux glaces* | *les glaces* |

# I can speak French

What do these mean?
Check on the pages shown.

Essaie-la.  23

S'il vous plaît.  6

Qu'est-ce que c'est?  22

J'ai le sac.  26

Je ne comprends pas.  22

Où est le cadeau?  18

Non, merci.  23

Veux-tu une glace?  8

Merci beaucoup.  15

Oui ou non?  24

Je ne peux pas.  13

Attendez une minute.  16

Vas-y.  23

Dis-le encore.  22

Je l'ai.  14

Can you find all these words in the pictures?

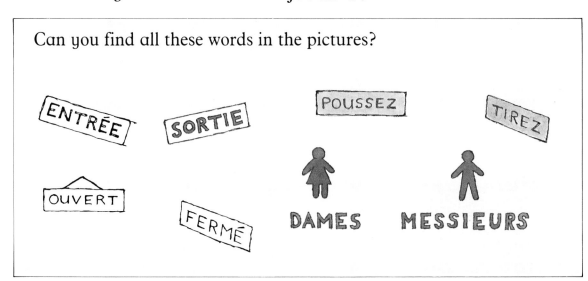

ENTRÉE   SORTIE   POUSSEZ   TIREZ

OUVERT   FERMÉ   DAMES   MESSIEURS

Did you know all the words?
When you do, you can make a badge to wear. Trace the badge on thin paper. Put your tracing on top of a sticky label.

Pressing hard, go over the shape and words again.

Colour the badge. Then cut it out and wear it with pride.

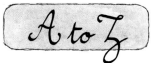

# Index and words to remember

**Aa**
*l'argent* money 4

**Bb**
*un billet* a ticket 6
*un bus* a bus 5

**Cc**
*un cadeau* a present 18
*une caméra* a camera
*cent* a hundred 20
*une chaise* a chair 12
*une chanson* a song
*un chien* a dog 11
*cinq* five 20
*cinquante* fifty 20
*un contrôleur* a bus driver/conductor

**Dd**
*une dame* a woman
*deux* two 6
*dix* ten 20

**Ee**
*une école* a school
*un enfant* a child

**Ff**
*une fille* a girl

**Gg**
*un garçon* a boy 22
*une glace* an ice-cream 8
*un gorille* a gorilla

**Hh**
*une heure* an hour
*un homme* a man
*huit* eight 20

**Ii**
*une invitation* an invitation

**Jj**
*un jeu* a game

**Kk**
*un kilomètre* a kilometre 20

**Ll**
*une laisse* a lead 13
*un livre* a book

**Mm**
*un magasin* a shop
*une minute* a minute 16
*un monsieur* a man

**Nn**

| | |
|---|---|
| *neuf* | nine 20 |
| *un numéro* | a number |

**Oo**

| | |
|---|---|
| *un oiseau* | a bird |

**Pp**

| | |
|---|---|
| *le pain* | bread |
| *une pâtisserie* | a cake shop 8 |
| *une photo* | a photo 16 |
| *un pied* | a foot 20 |
| *une piscine* | a swimming pool 5 |
| *un placard* | a cupboard/locker 14 |

**Qq**

| | |
|---|---|
| *quatre* | four 20 |
| *une question* | a question |

**Rr**

| | |
|---|---|
| *une rue* | a street |

**Ss**

| | |
|---|---|
| *un sac* | a bag 4 |
| *sept* | seven 20 |
| *six* | six 20 |
| *un ski* | a ski |
| *un soulier* | a shoe 20 |

**Tt**

| | |
|---|---|
| *une tête* | a head |
| *un train* | a train |
| *trois* | three 9 |

**Uu**

| | |
|---|---|
| *un* | one 6 |
| *une usine* | a factory |

**Vv**

| | |
|---|---|
| *un vélo* | a bike |

**Ww**

| | |
|---|---|
| *Un WC* | a toilet |

**Yy**

| | |
|---|---|
| *un yaourt* | a yogurt |

**Zz**

| | |
|---|---|
| *zéro* | nought |

# Making the best of this book

Children learn a language (including their own) by first hearing and understanding it, and then imitating it. To begin with, they pick up words and phrases – blocks of language – that they can use in everyday situations. At first their pronunciation and grammar may not be correct, but there's no need to 'get it right'. Children naturally change their speech, bit by bit, to get it closer to what they hear. That's how this book works.

Everyone enjoys success. Praise encourages children to learn more and more. Here are some useful words: *Bien! Très bien! Bravo*! If you can't speak French, it is better not to try to read the French because you may pronounce it wrong. Get the cassette or ask someone who knows French to read the book out loud for you. All the family can share in learning French at the same time.

Below we suggest ways that may help you use this book and get the best out of it. You will probably find many others, too.

## Steps to success

1 Get someone to read the story out loud in English. Then listen to the story on the cassette – or ask someone who speaks French to read it. Look at the pictures and listen carefully to the French.
   Listen to the ABC song on the cassette and point to the letters on pages 30/31.

2 Listen to the story again, following in the book and repeating the French words.
   Sing the ABC song again and play the game on page 18.

3 Listen to the story again. By now you can probably join in.
   Sing the ABC song again and play the game on page 19.

4 Say the numbers and listen to the kilometre song on the cassette. Look at the pictures on pages 20/21. You can march up and down like the three M's as you sing.

5 Look at the pictures on pages 22/23 and listen to what all the characters say on the cassette.

6 Listen to the rhymes and number chants on the cassette. Repeat them and follow the words on page 24. Can you remember the rhymes?

7 Make the puppets on page 25. Listen to the story again as you do so. Then make the puppets act. They can say the words on pages 22/23. They can sing the song on pages 20/21 and say the rhymes on page 24.

8 Make a puppet of the old lady and the bus conductor and act out the whole story. Get your friends to help you.

9 Get the puppets to play the games on pages 18/19. Sing the kilometre song with them.

10 See if you can 'say it right' with your puppets or with your friends (pages 26/27).

11 Did you find all the phrases and words on page 28? Do you know what they mean? Can you say them right?

12 Now you are speaking French. *Bravo! Bien! Très bien*! Make yourself a badge, and show off your French to your friends!